30 Days
To Stop Being A Shopaholic

A Mindfulness Program with a Touch of Humor

Harper Daniels

Copyright © JV 2020

This book is meant to be a guide only, and does not guarantee specific results. If the lessons and exercises in this book are followed, change can occur for certain people. Results vary from person to person; some people may not need to complete the thirty days to experience change, but it's encouraged that the entire program be read completely through at least once.

The last half of the book consists of blank note pages that the reader can use in conjunction with the exercises for each day. The reader is encouraged to utilize the note pages; though it's not necessary.

Give the gift of mindfulness. Consider giving one of our mindfulness workbooks to a loved one!

Disclosure (Shared Lessons and Exercises):
Keep in mind that our mindfulness guides share the same lessons and exercises, so there is no need to purchase more than one book; unless you are sharing with a group or giving the guides as gifts. Our mindfulness guides are created for various topics; however, they utilize the same lessons and exercises, so please be aware of this before purchasing. For example, *30 Days to Stop Being a Shopaholic* will mostly have the same lessons and exercises as *30 Days to Reduce Stress* and so forth. By reading just one of our guides, you'll be able to apply the same lessons and exercises to multiple areas of your life.

Enjoy your journey of self-discovery!

Contents

Preface..4

Day 1...7
Day 2...8
Day 3...9
Day 4..10
Day 5..11
Day 6..12
Day 7..13
Day 8..14
Day 9..15
Day 10..16
Day 11..17
Day 12..18
Day 13..19
Day 14..20
Day 15..21
Day 16..22
Day 17..23
Day 18..24
Day 19..25
Day 20..26
Day 21..27
Day 22..28
Day 23..29
Day 24..30
Day 25..31
Day 26..32
Day 27..33
Day 28..34
Day 29..35
Day 30..36

Conclusion..37
Note Pages...Begins on 39

Preface

If you're addicted to shopping, don't be alarmed. It's a common addiction in our modern and materialistic world. With advertisements bombarding our senses all day long, it can be difficult to escape the trap. This unique dependency is shared by many consumers; but you don't have to follow the crowd of addicted and needy customers any longer. Let this 30 day mindfulness program help you to overcome shopaholism, so that you can start living your best life possible in the present moment, free from the need to shop.

For the purpose of this book let's define *shopaholic* as: a person with an attachment to the misconception that spending and buying are necessary for present moment happiness. *Shopaholism* can be thought of as an attachment to the belief that the purchasing of material possessions establishes a coveted reputation, status, and identity. Feel free to define *shopaholic* and *shopaholism* any way you wish, as long as you recognize the problem as a dependency on an attachment that uses purchases to maintain an illusory existence. In other words, a shopaholic is addicted to the false belief that happiness can be bought.

The following pages involve a 30 day program made up of lessons and exercises to help you overcome ways of thinking that have kept you stuck as a shopaholic. Though these lessons and exercises can be applied to any unhealthy reliance, this program will focus specifically on the problem of compulsive shopping, which is unhealthy and destructive to your presence and awareness.

For some readers, they'll overcome the reliance quickly and will drop their unhealthy thoughts and shopaholism in no time; and for others, they'll overcome slowly and gradually. In either case, if you stick with the program you'll start to witness your shopaholism break. Please don't judge your progress in the program, as this isn't a competition and there isn't a goal you must attain. Let the adverse thoughts, feelings, behaviors, and habit simply drop as you work through the exercises and lessons.

It's not necessary to complete the program's days in order, nor should you be religious about completing them successfully. There is no such thing as a successful completion of this program. The bottom line is to observe and awaken, and that cannot be obtained through success, force, pressure, struggle, or competition. Simply relax, follow the program, and the grip of the dependency will loosen.

You'll also notice that mindfulness, silence, and stillness are a regular discipline for each day in the program. Because you've been influenced by a dependency based society that demands instant gratification, silence and stillness may seem nearly impossible for you to practice. For this reason, we'll incorporate this discipline from the outset. A quiet and still mind is an incredibly powerful resource, but one that requires daily maintenance.

It should also be noted that you're not required to stop shopping during this 30 day program. The point being: by practicing the following exercises and lessons in the days to come, you won't even need willpower to drop a shopaholic addiction.

One of the most important lessons to keep in mind is to not fight your shopaholism while participating in this program. Dependencies, addictions, and strong patterns of thinking are empowered by a fight and struggle. Continue shopping for the length of this program without regret or remorse; unless you have allowed the addiction to drop. Spending habits, like most adverse dependencies, feed on negative thought patterns, fear, and struggle. This program will help you overcome the attachment without conflict.

You'll need about 15-30 minutes per day for the program; but feel free to spend more time if needed. The amount of time doesn't matter, as long as you're in an environment that allows you to concentrate without distraction.

Also to be mentioned, the last 30 pages of this book are clear note pages that correspond to the 30 days. It's encouraged that you write down any thoughts, insights, adaptations, lessons, mantras, etc, on those pages. The note pages can also be used to rip out and take with you. Feel free to use them as you wish.

One last thing: If you're like most people, you might be dependent on caffeine, alcohol, or sugar to some extent. If you are, do your best to lessen the consumption of these substances over the next 30 days. It's not necessary that you abstain, but can you cut consumption of these substances in half, or more? It's important that your mind is sober and your body relaxed to make the most of these exercises and lessons.

Let's get started.

Day 1

Exercise:

Find a place without distraction, and turn off all electronics. Sit with your back straight, kneel, or lie on a hard surface (not bed) and remain in silence for 10 minutes.

During these 10 minutes, take deep and focused breaths and hold them for a few seconds each. Exhale slowly. Listen intently to your breathing. Don't try to change it — simply listen, and feel the air go in and out.

When you're ready, repeat the mantra: **"Be still. Be silent."** *Repeat this slowly multiple times out loud as well as quietly. You might experience boredom or anxiety, but continue repeating the mantra regardless. Repeat it until you're calm and focused. You can continue the deep breathing during the mantra, or take deep breaths during pauses. Don't rush.*

Each of the 30 days will have this time of silence, focused breathing, and a mantra. Except for this page, the end of each day will remind you of the minutes you are to spend in silence and focused breathing; and will also have a mantra for you to practice. You can repeat the mantras during your times of silence and focused breathing, or following. Remember, there is no right or wrong way to do this.

Addictions want to fight; in fact, they're energized by fighting. Instead of fighting shopaholism, meet it with silence and observation. Let the exercises and lessons in this program guide you.

Day 2

Exercise:

Ponder this question: Can you remember a time in your life when you weren't addicted to shopping?

Writing is extremely beneficial to the mind; especially when pondering. Write down your thoughts about this particular question. If your mind drifts, then write whatever thoughts emerge. It's okay if you have nothing to write, but ponder the question regardless.

Were you able to remember a period in your life when you weren't a shopaholic? If you're like many people, you may have to return to memories of childhood to determine that period. It's not uncommon for a person to learn to become a shopaholic at an early age. Shopaholics have often been influenced, supported, conditioned, motivated, and taught by other shopping addicts within society and family.

Recognize that being a shopaholic is a learned behavior with roots. However, this addiction can be dropped quickly and completely; and you have the capability to drop it.

*10 minutes of silence and focused breathing. Repeat the mantra: **"Drop. Unlearn. Discover."**

Day 3

Exercise:

On a piece of paper, write down all the labels and adjectives that you and others use to identify you.

For example, do you see yourself as a daughter, son, mother, father, student, teacher, cashier, friend, engineer, accountant, employee, employer, roommate, wife, husband, etc? And what adjectives do you use to label yourself; for example, do you identify yourself as failed, successful, happy, depressed, good, moral, unethical, lustful, greedy, valuable, worthless, etc? Don't only write down the labels and descriptions you perceive; but also write down what you believe others label you as: do you believe others see you as a valuable friend, stupid and incompetent employee, extremely smart and talented worker, etc? Take as long as you need, and fill up a sheet of paper with those labels and descriptions. *volunteer*

After you've done that, tear the paper into multiple pieces and throw it away. Those labels and adjectives mean nothing. They're not *you*. You cannot be defined, labeled, described, or controlled by titles. Most people poison their conscience with such learned vocabulary. They really believe these words hold power – they'll even fight, stress out, become ill, and die to make these words part of reality. Shopaholic dependencies, as well as most societal habits, teach you to identify with particular words, which are only thoughts. Unlearn them.

*10 minutes of silence and focused breathing. Repeat the mantra: **"I am not a label, title, or description."***
I am a fluid, always changing force.

Day 4

Exercise:

Count to 25 slowly, pausing for a few seconds before the next number; then, count backward from 25 slowly. Try this with your eyes closed. While counting up you can imagine yourself being lifted into the sky; and then while counting down, descending back to earth.

Our world today is about speed. Everyone seems to be in a rush, yet most people are unsatisfied; and, they have no clue where they're going. Chasing the next best thing is a fruitless endeavor. It's the rare person who slows down to enjoy the present moment, regardless of its nature. Because there seems to be so many problems, and most jobs are focused on resolving those problems, people are compelled to accept anxiety and rush toward a reward and conclusion. That surely isn't happiness. Happiness can only be found in the present moment, not in a hypothetical future of rewards and successes. Rushing is another form of going nowhere.

How many times have you rushed through shopping? This is destructive to your peace of mind, mental health, and body: concentration suffers, stress levels rise, blood pressure increases, and awareness to the present moment isn't possible.

It's critical to slow down. You only have one life to live – don't rush through it, and don't be dependent on anything that encourages you to rush. Be still, and slow down.

*10 minutes of silence and focused breathing. Repeat the mantra: "**Slow down. Do not rush. Enjoy the present moment.**"

Day 5

Exercise:

Choose a few adverse emotions that you frequently experience (anxiety, depression, shame, guilt, worry, anger, etc.)

Now, assign each emotion a person's name – choose names of people you don't know. For example, if you frequently experience worry, name the emotion "Charlie" (assuming you don't know anyone named Charlie). Do this for all the negative emotions you regularly experience.

This exercise is helpful for addressing common adverse emotions that show up frequently in your life. Instead of ignoring the emotion, call it by its new name and say, *"Hey Charlie, I see you're here again. You're not obligated to stay. It's nice having you around, but feel free to leave at any time."* You don't have to use that exact response, but you get the gist. Don't fight the feelings or thoughts that accompany it; just call the emotion by its new name and give it a funny greeting – you can even tell it to stick around because you plan on observing it.

If you practice this exercise often, you'll experience a great relief, because you're awakening to the fact that you are not your emotions. Negative emotions come and go if you let them. Shopaholism thrives on these emotions, so it's important to recognize them as separate from your being.

*10 minutes of silence and focused breathing. Repeat the mantra: **"The emotions I experience are free to go."**

Day 6

Exercise:

Observe your body. Observe how it feels, moves, and reacts. More direction is explained below.

If you're still caught up in shopaholism, observe your body movements, sounds, sensations, and breaths while being a shopaholic. Do your eyes look down or roll? Do you move your hands fast or slow? Does your voice rise or lower? How is your posture? Do you smile or frown? Try to observe everything about your body while shopping compulsively. Be aware of shopping's affect on your body.

If you are not being a shopaholic today, then continue with the 10 minutes of silence and focused breathing, but get in touch with your body. A good way to do this is by touching each body part and saying its name, leaving your hand on the part for a few seconds and feeling its texture and warmth. Start with your head: place your hand on your head and say, "*I am touching my head.*" And then work your way down to your shoulders, arms, stomach, legs, knees, and feet. Focus your attention on one body part at a time. Say its name and describe what you are touching.

*10 minutes of silence and focused breathing. Repeat the mantra: "***I am not my body.**"

Day 7

Exercise:

Say the words "Guilt", "Shame", and "Regret" 10 times to yourself out loud. Don't rush. Pause between each repetition. For the pause, you can take a deep breath. Your eyes can remain open or closed. Again, don't rush - say the words slowly and observe any thoughts, feelings, or images that emerge internally.

Now, say these words again 10 times, but with a smile.

What futile credence we give words such as Guilt, Shame and Regret. We use these words on ourselves as well as others; they become regular vocabulary for our internal recurring voices. And in the end, they're mere words that hold no power. What would these words be without a facial expression, tone, inflection, or emphasis?

When you said these three specific words, what thoughts came to mind, what did you feel, and was there a reaction in your body? If there is a reaction, such as shortness of breath or a frown, people tend to interpret it as sadness; but this reaction is a learned behavior. We've been taught to feel and think a certain way with regard to guilt, shame, and regret. The truth is: these words mean nothing.

Shopaholic behavior, like most dependencies, flourishes on these three words and the learned reactions they produce. But see them for what they are...mere words with no power.

*10 minutes of silence and focused breathing. Repeat the mantra: *"**I am not Guilt, Shame, or Regret.**"*

Day 8

Exercise:

Turn off your cell phone, or put it in airplane mode, for at least 1 hour, and observe the thoughts you experience. If you don't have any major responsibilities this day, or if you have all you need and don't require the phone, then turn off your cell phone for 12 hours. This exercise works best if you can go 24 hours without your cell phone activated; but go no less than 1 hour. If there are people who are immediately dependent on you, send them a text saying that you'll be unavailable, and then turn off your phone.

Like never before in history, we live in a modern world with a plethora of distractions. These distractions fight for our attention, because money is behind the scenes. Every business is wondering how they can break your distraction from one thing so that you can be distracted by their thing. It's a constant war between everyone; and the businesses that can influence the most shopaholics, wins. Whoever can hold your attention the longest, wins the battle; but whoever can make you dependent, wins the war. The smartphone has become a primary channel for these businesses to influence shopaholic behavior.

Shopaholic dependent companies need for you to be distracted by their business; otherwise you might wake up to reality and enjoy the beauty of life, which includes living happily in the present moment. Shopaholism has made its way into smartphones, and companies want you to become the most dependent shopaholic out there; so power off your phone.

*10 minutes of silence and focused breathing. Repeat the mantra: **"*I am not distracted. I am here and now.*"**

Day 9

Exercise:

On a piece of paper (any size) write down the goals that you've been striving to achieve – i.e. the goals that you believe will bring you fulfillment. For example: a new job, a house in a nice neighborhood, traveling the world, a business, a family, new friends, a degree or certification, building a network, reaching a net worth of a million dollars, etc.

Now, tear up the paper into multiple pieces and throw away.

Goals can be very helpful and useful if they're not obsessed over. However, in the modern world people develop a reliance on goals. Think about all the times you've said something like, "*I need to get that,*" "*I must reach this,*" "*I'll do anything to accomplish that*", etc. It's often the case that people spend more time worrying about their goals, than freely doing something in the present moment to reach them. Plus, the goal in itself is fleeting, while the journey in the present moment is real and lasting.

The habit of thinking that goals must be met, or else failure ensues, is subtly fixed to dependencies. When you've compulsively shopped in the past, what was the goal? What was it that you felt you needed to achieve?

*10 minutes of silence and focused breathing. Repeat the mantra: **"My happiness does not depend on meeting a goal. I'm happy now."**

Day 10

Exercise:

Go out and buy a small trash can. You should be able to find one cheaply. If you don't have the funds for this exercise, you can use an empty box or container; however, a small trash can works better for its symbolism.

Designate this specific trash can your "concerns and worries can" (or use any title you wish) – some people benefit from writing this label directly onto the can.

Now, write down (on scraps of paper or whatever paper you wish to use) any concerns, worries, and adverse thoughts that you may be experiencing today, and throw them into the can. Try to practice this every day: quickly write down worries, concerns, and negative thoughts, and then throw them into the can. It may be beneficial to have a supply of scrap paper near the can for easy access.

This exercise may seem simple, but let's go beyond throwing your written concerns, worries, and thoughts away. Designate a few times during the week for sifting through the can and taking out random worries and concerns from days prior – just reach in and pull some out. Observe them, but don't judge yourself. This is a great exercise to learn your negative thought patterns and the lies that grip your conscience. If you stick with this practice, you may gain a deeper understanding into the dependencies, habits, thought patterns, and feelings that have you stuck as a shopaholic.

*10 minutes of silence and focused breathing. Repeat the mantra: **"There is nothing to worry about. All is well."**

Day 11

Exercise:

Write a letter or email to yourself. There is something about using pen and paper that is very effective when writing letters, but feel free to write an email if you wish. Don't send the letter or email, just write it and save it for a day – you can toss it out or delete it tomorrow.

Write anything that comes to mind: It can be advice you want to give yourself, a story from the past, random thoughts and feelings, frustrations and worries, things you're thankful for, etc. There is no right or wrong – write whatever comes to mind in the moment. Try to write at least two full paragraphs.

What was the theme and voice of your message? Was it a positive or negative tone? Were you advising yourself? Did you make any judgments about yourself? Did you start demanding that you should or should not do something? Was the letter full of gratitude? Was there anger and despair? Read the letter as if you were reading it from a friend – is it a letter that would upset you, or one that you would welcome with excitement and a smile?

Whatever you wrote is essentially being written on the tablet of your mind. This exercise is useful for getting to know the internal voice that we all have in our minds. It's an internal voice that can change for the better with observation, acceptance, and awareness. Be aware of your internal voice in the present moment.

*10 minutes of silence and focused breathing. Repeat the mantra: *"I am not my internal voice. I am aware."*

Day 12

Exercise:

Spend 5 minutes smelling something aromatic: a piece of fruit, a spice, tea, pine, cedar, a flower, a scented candle, etc. Focus on the smell of that one thing for the entire 5 minutes. Don't let anything distract you from the smell.

How often do you take time to enjoy a fragrant smell? One of the lies of modern society is that if you stop and enjoy your five senses for too long, you'll miss out on…fill in the blank. While people are rushing toward their goals with stress levels spiking, they're totally missing out on awareness in the present moment. People stare at images of food that others have posted on the internet, but don't take the time to smell or taste real food in the present moment.

What's better: shopping, or enjoying the smell of vanilla, orange, or pine in the present moment? The first is a fake and illusory pleasure; the second is real and sensational. Shopaholism does a great job from stealing time and energy from your other senses, such as smell. One of the best ways get into the present moment and away from an illusion is through focusing on smell and the use of your other senses. Don't let shopaholism diminish your other senses any longer.

*10 minutes of silence and focused breathing. Repeat the mantra: **"I can sense the present."**

Day 13

Exercise:

Taste something by eating it very slowly for at least 5 minutes. Pick something with a lot of flavor: a piece of fruit, a strong tea, a spice, soup with many ingredients, honey, etc. Close your eyes through most of your tasting. Savor the piece of food slowly. Pay close attention to the feel of the taste on your tongue. Chew slowly.

As mentioned yesterday, shopaholism does a great job at stealing presence away from the other senses, as do many dependencies. Since shopaholism is directly related to our security senses, the more those senses are abused the more our other senses are neglected. When was the last time you thoroughly enjoyed the taste of an orange, vanilla, dark chocolate, olive oil, or cheese? I don't mean enjoying the flavor for a few seconds and then continuing on to eat, but to let the flavor linger before taking another bite.

The taste of a pineapple, pepper, grape, or apple is far more real and satisfying than shopping. It may sound silly to say that, but it's true, because those foods are based in reality. You can actually interact with them in the present, and they don't hypnotize you into an illusory fake relationship like shopaholism attempts to do.

Let the taste of food bring you into the present moment, and away from shopaholism.

*10 minutes of silence and focused breathing. Repeat the mantra: *"I am free to taste."*

Day 14

Exercise:

This exercise may seem frivolous, but give it a try; because it may be one of the lessons that benefit you most.

For the remainder of the day, whenever you use the bathroom, for any reason, take your time with what you're doing. Don't rush through the process, like you may normally do. Focus on taking your time in the bathroom; do every step of your bathroom experience twice as slow. It may even help to say each step: "I am now sitting up straight on the toilet," "I am now putting soap on my hands," "I am now drying my hands," etc.

Most people hurry up their bathroom experience, not realizing what they're doing – forcing, not standing or sitting straight, not relaxing, not washing their hands properly, not drying their hands slowly. They rush in and out, like they have somewhere important to go. Don't be like that any longer. Take your time in the bathroom; it's not only unhealthy for the body to rush the excretion process, but it's also unhealthy for the mind. A rushed bathroom experience doesn't allow you to live in the present moment. Allow the excretion and cleaning to happen naturally with relaxed and focused attention.

The patterns of thinking as a shopaholic require rushing, worrying, and hurrying. Slow down considerably, and the shopaholism will drop.

*10 minutes of silence and focused breathing. Repeat the mantra: **"Don't hurry. Stay present. Stay still."**

Day 15

Exercise:

Compliment a total stranger today. You can compliment a cashier, service provider over the phone, server, barista, person at the gym or grocery store, someone on the bus or train, or whomever. It's best if you are not attracted to the person in any way. Compliment someone that you normally wouldn't compliment.

For many people, kindness doesn't come easy. We are taught to judge and avoid from a very early age. You may be a kind person with a good heart; but you're fooling yourself if you believe you treat everyone the same. Spend a few moments today complimenting people you normally wouldn't - not because you dislike them, but because they escape your radar for whatever reason.

It feels good to compliment people, especially when they're overlooked, excluded, and not normally on your radar. As a shopaholic, shopaholism can often impede the natural inclination to treat people respectfully. Shopaholism has a way of blinding us from the people in our present moment experience. Make it a point to compliment people every day with a genuine heart and loving attitude.

Kindness is a self healer. Shopaholism can't survive in the presence of genuine kindness.

*10 minutes of silence and focused breathing. Repeat the mantra: ***"Kindness heals."***

Day 16

Exercise:

Choose a song to listen to carefully. You can choose the song from your music collection; or simply turn on the radio and wait for a song to play.

While listening to the song, don't listen to the notes, beats, voice, or rhythm; instead, listen for the silence between sounds. Listen for the stops, pauses, and absence of sound between notes. Listen for the silence in the song.

Have you ever realized that your favorite songs would not exist without silence? Every note, rhythm, beat, and voice needs a moment of silence to manifest – even if that moment exists in a millisecond. Without silence, there would be no noise, yet alone music. This isn't to say that noise and silence are in conflict; quite the opposite actually. Sounds and silence are complementary. So, were you able to hear the silence within the song? Practice this repeatedly whenever you listen to music. Listen for the silence that allows the music to endure.

Similarly, we need silence in order to let the rhythm of life manifest. Unfortunately, this has become a struggle for many people, because we live in an unbalanced world that encourages sound over silence. Don't follow noise dependent crowds, and don't fear silence. Silence is a powerful remedy. Practice remaining in silence daily; you'll start to hear and see new and wonderful things.

*15 minutes of silence and focused breathing. Repeat the mantra: **"Be silent. Listen. Be silent."**

Day 17

Exercise:

On a sheet of paper (one that you can easily save and return to later) make a list of hobbies that you've had in the past but have neglected, and also make a list of hobbies that you would like to start in the future.

From these lists choose one hobby from the past and one new hobby that you'd like to start. Focus only on these two – the old hobby and the new one. Make this a priority.

How often have you said, or have heard other people say, *"I wish I had the time."* You do have the time. You just choose to think of time in the way that you've been taught to perceive it. If your life depended on it, you would certainly make the time if needed.

In fact, time is a manmade construct - don't ever forget that. There is only the present moment. Past and future are not here and now. We spend far too much time thinking about time. How many of your recurrent inner thoughts involve questions such as, *"When will that ever happen?"* *"When will I ever change?"* *"Why did that have to happen?"* *"If I can buy more things, life will be better."* These are lies that only eat into the present moment, and infect our modern world.

Shopaholic habits, patterns of thinking, and behavior occupy the present moment; and that moment could be used to pursue hobbies that magnify your happiness.

*15 minutes of silence and focused breathing. Repeat the mantra: ***"The time is now. Happiness is present."***

Day 18

Exercise:

Lay down on the floor (not on a bed or couch), with your back straight and your arms at your side. Close your eyes.

Now, imagine yourself in a coffin or under the ground. If this depresses you, do it regardless. With your eyes closed, imagine not being able to open them ever again; also imagine not being able to move your body or speaking ever again. Stay in this position for 10 minutes, or as long as you can.

If this seems gothic or dark, that's only your learned perception of the death experience. There's an ancient teaching that says the way to enlightenment is through a keen awareness of death. The person who is daily reminded that the body will die, and faces this fact head on with a clear mind and acceptance, has nothing to lose and is truly free to live in the present moment. The question isn't whether or not your body will die (because it surely will); the more important question is will you live before death?

Will you truly live before your body dies? The present moment is the only thing you'll always experience. Instead of fearing a pending death, accept it and be thankful for the present moment, and live in it! Don't spend the present moment being a shopaholic any longer. Life is beautiful, start living in the present moment without shopaholism.

*15 minutes of silence and focused breathing. Repeat the mantra: **"My body will age and pass, but I will always be present."**

Day 19

Exercise:

This exercise will require a bit of courage. If you believe it'll cause too much anxiety, then there will be an alternative below. Assuming it is warmer weather, put on a shirt backward and go to a public place (store, park, movie theater, walk around the block, etc). If it's colder weather, go to a public place wearing your hat inside out, two different shoes or boots, or a jacket inside out. In other words, go into a public place dressed in a piece of clothing that is worn oddly or wrong.

If you can't, or won't, do this; then wear a shirt backwards around your home until you go to bed.

What thoughts and feelings did you experience during this exercise? Did your behavior change in any way, or your interaction with people? Did changing the way you wore clothing change you? People put a lot of worry, concern, and thought into what they wear. Judgments abound in certain societies that consider clothing a necessity for identity; and just like many societal customs, clothing trends and styles change.

If you identify with your clothing, you'll remain unaware of yourself in the present moment. Wear clothes, but don't let clothing cover your true being; experience the present moment without the hindrance of apparel, fashion, or style.

*15 minutes of silence and focused breathing. Repeat the mantra: **"I am not a style or brand. I am a free being."**

Day 20

Exercise:

Imagine this scenario: It is 3:00 AM. You wake up and realize that your home is on fire. Everyone, except you, is out of the house. You realize that you only have a minute or less to get yourself out before everything is destroyed. You must act immediately.

With such a short amount of time, what do you grab to take with you?

Really consider this scenario; because it happens to people every day around the world. People are forced to leave their homes because of fire, flood, violence, and other uncontrollable factors. If this happened to you, what physical things would you grab and take in such a short window of time? Your cell phone, book, family pictures, computer, passport, specific files, a project, particular article of clothing, or nothing at all? Whatever you take within that moment will be the most meaningful objects to you. What does your answer tell you about your desires, attachments, concerns, needs, and habits?

Most shopaholics are shopping for things of little value or worth, when considering the bigger picture. Identify what specific objects in your current possession have the most value and worth to you. More than likely, the last thing you shopped for probably won't be of much value to you if your house is burning down.

*15 minutes of silence and focused breathing. Repeat the mantra: "*I am not my possessions. I am free from material things.*"*

Day 21

Exercise:

Choose a physical symbol that will remind you to observe and be aware in the present moment. Try to choose something from nature, or that is made of natural material.

The object you choose can be anything, but it's best if it's something that you can enjoy looking at and touching. For example, many walkers and hikers will find a unique rock small enough to carry in their hands. A stone, necklace, bracelet, seashell, cedar block, coin…anything will do, as long as you enjoy it and you can dedicate it as a tool for remembrance.

Another cunning trick of shopaholic behavior is to confuse the mind into forgetting you're part of the natural world. Shopaholic tendencies require you to use the imagination, which can be easily manipulated for the business of being a shopaholic. Thus, you're taken out of physical reality. By having a symbol of remembrance, you can reconnect with the present moment. This symbol isn't meant to be an idol, god, or icon. Don't think too deeply into this. The symbol is simply a tool to help you remember where you are in the *here and now*. As long as you're aware of the present, you'll have no desire to return to the hallucination of shopaholism.

*15 minutes of silence and focused breathing. Repeat the mantra: *"**All is well. Here and now, all is well.**"*

Day 22

Exercise:

Hold a smile for 5 minutes. You don't need to do this exercise in front of a mirror; but feel free to do so if you wish. You can even do this exercise during the 15 minutes of silence and focused breathing. While holding your smile, take a moment and feel your face; actually touch the smile and the curvature of your lips and cheek bones.

Have you ever behaved a certain way and then saw your mood change immediately? Physical exercise, such as running and weightlifting, does this for many people. Certain forms of yoga have also been used by people to change their moods. The point is: changing your behavior not only impacts other people, but can also impact your perception of yourself.

You'll notice that while you're smiling during this exercise, you may experience certain emotions. You might feel silly, embarrassed, weird, or stupid. Continue smiling regardless. In fact, if you are still being a shopaholic at this point in the program, smile while you're in shopaholic mode – hold the smile until you are through experiencing shopaholism; set an alarm if needed. As always, observe your thoughts while you're smiling; observe the thoughts as if they're clouds passing by in a bright blue sky.

Smiling causes an authentic reaction in our bodies and minds that is essentially good. The present moment enjoys a nice smile. So hold that smile until you no longer can.

*15 minutes of silence and focused breathing. Repeat the mantra: **"Happiness is now. I am happy."**

Day 23

Exercise:

Focus on a natural object or scene for 10 minutes, without distraction and in silence.

Focusing on a natural object for an extended period of time is an ancient practice. How often have you stopped to observe something objectively for more than 10 minutes? When was the last time you've quietly watched a sunset, sunrise, tree sway in the wind, bird chirping, clouds passing or expanding, or just a rock? That might sound boring, but this practice is very liberating. If you look at anything long enough you start to see it from a different perspective. As easy as this exercise sounds, it's not – try it out, and see how long you can observe without thoughts impeding the practice.

Watching a bird feed may be more interesting than watching an immobile rock; but I encourage you to start with an immobile object, such as a stone or piece of wood. During this process thoughts will emerge – observe the thoughts and let them pass. Don't attach a goal or benchmark of success to this exercise; just observe an object.

Shopaholism wants to hypnotize you with a false narrative; stealing your attention from the present moment. Refocus on the here and now. Silent observation is essential.

*15 minutes of silence and focused breathing. Repeat the mantra: **"Be focused. Observe. Be present."**

Day 24

Exercise:

Pinch the skin on the back of your hand or forearm until there is discomfort and slight pain. It's not necessary to pinch hard enough to bruise yourself, just enough to feel a small burn.

Did I cause the pain by asking you to do this exercise? No; you caused this pain to yourself – think about this carefully. You even decided how much pain to give yourself, and when to relieve the pain. You can't blame me or anyone else for the pain you just experienced. You were solely responsible. You were also responsible for letting go.

This is easily understood with regard to physical pain, such as pinching oneself; however, we have a lot of difficulty understanding this lesson as it applies to adverse emotions and feelings. How often have you said, and have heard others say, *"He makes me so angry when..."*, *"I'm depressed because she..."*, or *"I'm so frustrated that they..."* No person ever makes you experience negative feelings. It's always you who are experiencing them; and then placing the blame on others. Essentially, you are emotionally pinching yourself and not letting go. People go their entire lives without releasing the pinch. Instead of letting go, they scream at others, *"Release the pain! Let go! Fix this! Stop this! You're to blame!"* Wake up and see that you are solely responsible for letting go of the pain, and you can do it now.

*15 minutes of silence and focused breathing. Repeat the mantra: **"I can release negative feelings, here and now."**

Day 25

Exercise:

Light a candle and observe its flame for 5 minutes. Watch it move and feel its heat. Appreciate its energy.

Now, blow out the flame.

(If you don't have a candle, light a match and blow it out; and if you don't have a candle or match, stare at a dim light for 5 minutes and then turn it off.)

The temperature of a small candle flame (and match flame) is around 1200 Celsius (which is about 2000 Fahrenheit). That's a lot of energy! And within a fraction of a second, it was extinguished as you blew it out; or in the case of the light, turned off its energy source. There wasn't a gradual process with delays and stops. You blew out the highly energized flame, and that was it - from 1200 Celsius to nonexistent in no time; or should I say, in present no time.

We think that our dependencies have so much energy and power. It's not just shopaholism; all adverse dependencies survive on this deception of power. The truth is: addictive attachments don't have energy like the candle flame, though your mind may have been tricked into believing they do. The candle flame is real and powerful; whereas dependencies are illusory and fictitious.

As easily and quickly as you extinguished the flame, you can drop shopaholism in the present moment.

*15 minutes of silence and focused breathing. Repeat the mantra: **"Dependency isn't real. It can be extinguished."***

Day 26

Exercise:

Go for a mindfulness walk for at least 10 minutes. Focus on each step. Feel the steps: the feel of your feet hitting the ground, your heel rolling forward, your toes, the bend of your knees, your hips working to balance your posture, the swinging of your arms, etc. Don't rush; go slow. Focus on your breathing as well. Get in tune with your body. Pay attention to your physical senses throughout the walk. Focus – don't listen to music or be distracted.

Human beings have always used walking as a naturally restorative exercise. There is something about walking, and focusing on the walk, that calms the mind and soul. The longer one walks, the more relaxed one feels.

Any moment is a good time to walk and experience your inner and outer environment. During long walks, thoughts will emerge that will allow you to consciously observe them. Let the thoughts pass; you may even have emotions that emerge, observe those and let them pass as well. Focusing on your steps will help you clear the mind of clutter. Walking in the early morning and at dusk is especially beneficial.

A 20 minute walk brings more comfort, stillness, peace, focus, and awareness than thousands of hours of shopping. Walk every day, as much as you can.

*15 minutes of silence and focused breathing. Repeat the mantra: **"I am relaxed. I am at peace."**

Day 27

Exercise:

On a sheet of paper (any size) write down all the internal lies that you regularly hear about yourself – i.e. within your mind.

Now, tear the paper into multiple pieces, and throw away.

It's common to have an internal voice (or voices) within your mind, playing a record of lies over and over. We eventually begin to accept these lies and let them impact our growth and happiness. Most people you see on a daily basis have these recurring internal voices; and most people are oblivious to them – sort of like white noise. This isn't a mental illness, but a way in which the mind works. We all experience these internal quiet voices whispering untruths about our being. These lies are nothing to fear, but they need to be observed. Writing them down can help you observe and become aware of their deceptions.

The power of silence, focused breathing, and mantras, which you have been practicing, is to draw out the lies. Let them manifest, and observe them. Common internal lies include: *"You are a loser," "You have become nothing, and you will never improve," "You are worthless. No one likes you," "You'll always be alone," "You're a burden,"* and so on. These thoughts are not part of you; however, the deception is to make you believe they are. Like many things in our culture, shopaholic patterns of thinking and behavior implant many of these lies clandestinely.

*15 minutes of silence and focused breathing. Repeat the mantra: **"Thoughts are only thoughts - nothing more."**

Day 28

Exercise:

Think of a major worry that consistently upsets you. On a sheet of paper, write down three worst case scenarios for that dominating concern. For example, if someone is persistently worried about dying alone, that individual can write as a worst case scenario, "I will die alone, without anyone at my side, and without family or loved ones to say goodbye." As mentioned, write down three worst case scenarios for the worry. The worry doesn't have to be as extreme as dying alone; use whichever worry hinders you.

Now, next to each of those three worst case scenarios write, "I accept this." You can either toss the paper or keep it.

Worry is an illness that goes untreated in most people. Think of worry like a cancer of the spirit; but few people know how to treat it effectively. One of the only ways to eradicate worry isn't to fight, ignore, or run from it; but to face it in the present moment and accept it for the illusion it is. You can never be worried about something happening in the present moment – that's impossible; you can only be worried about the future, which is always illusory.

Writing down your worries and worst case scenarios, if they ever do come true (which they rarely do), is a great way to draw those thoughts out of your mind and into the present moment, allowing you to face, accept, and observe them. This is much more effective than shopping.

*15 minutes of silence and focused breathing. Repeat the mantra: **"Worries are not real. They are passing thoughts."**

Day 29

Exercise:

Make yourself laugh for 5 minutes. Don't stop laughing. You might feel strange, weird, embarrassed, or stupid...it doesn't matter, just laugh. Try to laugh alone and without the aid of a comedy or joke. If you don't know how to start, just start making the noises that typically accompany your laughter.

What feelings did you experience during this exercise? Many people report feeling embarrassed or goofy, which is great; however, most people also report a feeling of relief and buoyancy when they've completed this exercise.

Similar to holding a smile, laughing for 5 minutes is a fantastic way to come into present awareness. If you think about it, humor is necessary for life. How sad is the person who is unable to laugh at the experiences of life? After all, life is funny, even the dreadful and lousy experiences.

If you ever again experience adverse thoughts and feelings of shopaholism, simply laugh at them. Consider how absurd and frivolous it is being a shopaholic; it really is a funny state of being. No other living thing on the planet becomes dependent on obtaining and possessing things. The entire situation is comical. If you perceive the shopaholic thoughts and behaviors for what they truly are - fictitious, impractical, and frivolous attachments – then they can be easily dropped. You must learn to laugh. Genuinely laugh the shopaholic tendencies away.

*15 minutes of silence and focused breathing. Repeat the mantra: **"Life is wonderful, funny, and real."**

Day 30

Exercise:

Take a piece of paper (one that you can keep) and write down all that you are grateful for – these things don't have to be in any particular order of importance.

Next to each thing you list, write "Thank you."

The person who isn't thankful for all that life gives is typically quite miserable; and shopaholics thrive on that misery. The truly grateful person can let go of anything at anytime. A thankful person is always a happy person, so practice gratitude daily.

Have you ever heard anyone say, *"I'm so grateful for being a shopaholic"*? Nobody is thankful for being a shopaholic; which is a clear sign that it's a destructive dependency. However, a few people have learned to be thankful for the present moment experience.

Not only is it unhealthy, but shopaholism discourages a grateful mind and soul. With only one life to live in the present moment, it's important to always emphasize a grateful heart. Spend time with people who are grateful, and do things that nourish a thankful heart in the present moment. Anything that encourages misery and depression isn't worth giving attention to. Be thankful, always.

*15 minutes of silence and focused breathing. Repeat the mantra: *"I am grateful. I am thankful."*

Conclusion

The exercises and lessons in this program taught and encouraged observation, awareness to your present moment experience, change of perception, and awakening to true happiness, which can only be found here and now. You were shown that your negative thoughts and feelings are not caused by shopaholism, or any unhealthy reliance, but are solely within you and illusory; which means that you are capable of letting those shopaholic thoughts and feelings pass and dropping the illusion of being a shopaholic.

As mentioned at the beginning, there were no goals or measures of success for this program. If you were hoping to find a reason to stop or continue being a shopaholic, then you may be spending too much time struggling and thinking. This was not meant to be a struggle, but a release.

Life is not meant to be spent being a shopaholic, or relying on any type of toxic behavior or pattern of thinking. Wake up to the present moment and enjoy your present experience. If you've made it through the program, you are certainly more awakened then when you started; however, don't give up mindfully practicing observation of thoughts and feelings, stillness, silence, deep and focused breathing, allowing everything to pass, laughing, smiling, and being grateful.

Live wonderfully awakened and aware.

Don't forget to leave a review and mention your favorite mindfulness exercise!

Notes for Day 1

(Use the space below to write down thoughts, reminders, ideas, new mantras, revelations, lessons, modifications to the exercise, experiences, etc.)

(40)

Notes for Day 2

(Use the space below to write down thoughts, reminders, ideas, new mantras, revelations, lessons, modifications to the exercise, experiences, etc.)

Notes for Day 3

(Use the space below to write down thoughts, reminders, ideas, new mantras, revelations, lessons, modifications to the exercise, experiences, etc.)

Notes for Day 4

(Use the space below to write down thoughts, reminders, ideas, new mantras, revelations, lessons, modifications to the exercise, experiences, etc.)

Notes for Day 5

(Use the space below to write down thoughts, reminders, ideas, new mantras, revelations, lessons, modifications to the exercise, experiences, etc.)

Notes for Day 6

(Use the space below to write down thoughts, reminders, ideas, new mantras, revelations, lessons, modifications to the exercise, experiences, etc.)

Notes for Day 7

(Use the space below to write down thoughts, reminders, ideas, new mantras, revelations, lessons, modifications to the exercise, experiences, etc.)

Notes for Day 8

(Use the space below to write down thoughts, reminders, ideas, new mantras, revelations, lessons, modifications to the exercise, experiences, etc.)

Notes for Day 9

(Use the space below to write down thoughts, reminders, ideas, new mantras, revelations, lessons, modifications to the exercise, experiences, etc.)

Notes for Day 10

(Use the space below to write down thoughts, reminders, ideas, new mantras, revelations, lessons, modifications to the exercise, experiences, etc.)

Notes for Day 11

(Use the space below to write down thoughts, reminders, ideas, new mantras, revelations, lessons, modifications to the exercise, experiences, etc.)

Notes for Day 12

(Use the space below to write down thoughts, reminders, ideas, new mantras, revelations, lessons, modifications to the exercise, experiences, etc.)

Notes for Day 13

(Use the space below to write down thoughts, reminders, ideas, new mantras, revelations, lessons, modifications to the exercise, experiences, etc.)

Notes for Day 14

(Use the space below to write down thoughts, reminders, ideas, new mantras, revelations, lessons, modifications to the exercise, experiences, etc.)

Notes for Day 15

(Use the space below to write down thoughts, reminders, ideas, new mantras, revelations, lessons, modifications to the exercise, experiences, etc.)

(68)

Notes for Day 16

(Use the space below to write down thoughts, reminders, ideas, new mantras, revelations, lessons, modifications to the exercise, experiences, etc.)

(70)

Notes for Day 17

(Use the space below to write down thoughts, reminders, ideas, new mantras, revelations, lessons, modifications to the exercise, experiences, etc.)

Notes for Day 18

(Use the space below to write down thoughts, reminders, ideas, new mantras, revelations, lessons, modifications to the exercise, experiences, etc.)

Notes for Day 19

(Use the space below to write down thoughts, reminders, ideas, new mantras, revelations, lessons, modifications to the exercise, experiences, etc.)

Notes for Day 20

(Use the space below to write down thoughts, reminders, ideas, new mantras, revelations, lessons, modifications to the exercise, experiences, etc.)

Notes for Day 21

(Use the space below to write down thoughts, reminders, ideas, new mantras, revelations, lessons, modifications to the exercise, experiences, etc.)

Notes for Day 22

(Use the space below to write down thoughts, reminders, ideas, new mantras, revelations, lessons, modifications to the exercise, experiences, etc.)

Notes for Day 23

(Use the space below to write down thoughts, reminders, ideas, new mantras, revelations, lessons, modifications to the exercise, experiences, etc.)

Notes for Day 24

(Use the space below to write down thoughts, reminders, ideas, new mantras, revelations, lessons, modifications to the exercise, experiences, etc.)

Notes for Day 25

(Use the space below to write down thoughts, reminders, ideas, new mantras, revelations, lessons, modifications to the exercise, experiences, etc.)

Notes for Day 26

(Use the space below to write down thoughts, reminders, ideas, new mantras, revelations, lessons, modifications to the exercise, experiences, etc.)

Notes for Day 27

(Use the space below to write down thoughts, reminders, ideas, new mantras, revelations, lessons, modifications to the exercise, experiences, etc.)

Notes for Day 28

(Use the space below to write down thoughts, reminders, ideas, new mantras, revelations, lessons, modifications to the exercise, experiences, etc.)

Notes for Day 29

(Use the space below to write down thoughts, reminders, ideas, new mantras, revelations, lessons, modifications to the exercise, experiences, etc.)

Notes for Day 30

(Use the space below to write down thoughts, reminders, ideas, new mantras, revelations, lessons, modifications to the exercise, experiences, etc.)

(98)

Made in the USA
Las Vegas, NV
25 June 2023

73873500R00059